Let Freedom Ring

The Louisiana Purchase

by Elizabeth D. Jaffe

Consultant:
Alecia P. Long, Ph.D.
Historian
Louisiana State Museum
New Orleans, Louisiana

Bridgestone Books
an imprint of Capstone Press
Mankato, Minnesota

Bridgestone Books are published by Capstone Press
151 Good Counsel Drive • P.O. Box 669 • Mankato, Minnesota 56002
http://www.capstone-press.com

Printed in the United States of America

Library of Congress Cataloging-in-Publication Data
Jaffe, Elizabeth Dana.
     The Louisiana Purchase / by Elizabeth D. Jaffe.
         p. cm. — (Let freedom ring)
     Includes bibliographical references and index.
     Summary: Explains the events that led Napoleon Bonaparte to sell the Louisiana
     Territory and the difficulties that Thomas Jefferson had in making the purchase that
     doubled the size of the United States.
     ISBN 0-7368-1100-1
     1. Louisiana Purchase—Juvenile literature. 2. United States—Territorial expansion—
Juvenile literature. [1. Louisiana Purchase. 2. United States—Territorial expansion.]
I. Title. II. Series.
E333 .J34 2002
973.4′6—dc21   2001005827

Editorial Credits
Rebecca Aldridge, editor; Kia Bielke, cover designer, interior layout designer, and interior
illustrator; Jennifer Schonborn, cover production designer; Deirdre Barton, photo researcher

Photo Credits
Cover: Bettman/CORBIS (middle, right), Stockbyte (left); Stockbyte, 4, 12, 16, 24, 28, 36;
Hulton/Archive Photos, 5, 9, 10–11, 30–31; North Wind Picture Archives, 6, 13, 21;
Giraudon/Art Resource, NY, 15; Reunion des Musees Nationaux/Art Resource, NY, 17;
Scala/Art Resource, NY, 18–19; Stock Montage, Inc., 22, 25, 26; Bettmann/CORBIS, 29, 33
(left), 37, 42; CORBIS, 33 (right); Joseph Sohm, ChromoSohm Inc./CORBIS, 38; Capstone
Press/Gary Sundermeyer, 40; PhotoSphere, 43

1   2   3   4   5   6   07   06   05   04   03   02

Table of Contents

Chapter One

Useless Land

One day in April 1803, Napoleon Bonaparte was soaking in a perfumed bath. Powerful Napoleon, the military ruler of France, had a goal to conquer and rule the world. As he relaxed in his tub, he thought about selling French land in North America called Louisiana.

Joseph and Lucien, Napoleon's brothers, interrupted his bath. They scolded their brother for the idea of selling Louisiana. Napoleon became angry. In a fit, Napoleon jumped up and splashed back down into the tub, soaking Joseph. A screaming match began among the brothers. One bathroom servant fainted from the strong argument.

Napoleon's enormous pride led him to do whatever he wanted to do. And it was Napoleon's decision that would help shape the United States into the sizable country it is today.

Napoleon Bonaparte ruled France from 1799 to 1815. His decision to sell the Louisiana Territory helped the United States become a larger and stronger nation.

New Land for France

On April 9, 1682, a group of French explorers stood near the mouth of the Mississippi River at the Gulf of Mexico. They had just finished a four-month journey down the Mississippi. People from Spain had been in this territory 150 years earlier. But they never claimed the land. The French explorers' leader, René Robert Cavelier, Sieur de La Salle, placed a cross at the river's mouth. By this action, La Salle claimed the land along the Mississippi for

By placing a cross at the mouth of the Mississippi River, La Salle (in red coat) claimed the land along the river for France.

René Robert Cavelier, Sieur de La Salle

La Salle continued on expeditions, or travels, after claiming Louisiana for France. In 1687, however, the men who worked and traveled with him murdered him.

France. He named the territory Louisiana, after the French king, Louis XIV.

Louis XIV was not interested in Louisiana. He had only one reason for encouraging French citizens to colonize land he considered "useless." His reason was to keep Britain, a powerful enemy nation, from settling there. Forty-five people from France settled the first permanent colony in Louisiana. Colonists who came later included fur trappers, people who traded with American Indians, boatmen, and farmers. Many French colonists settled in or near the port of New Orleans or in villages along the Mississippi.

The French and Indian War

By 1754, only about 2,000 French people lived in Louisiana. British colonists began settling in the

New Orleans

New Orleans was an important city that the French settled in 1718. They established the city to control use of the Mississippi River and prevent Spain and Britain from using it. Many products passed by ship across the Atlantic Ocean through New Orleans. Some of the products included flour, tobacco, pork, bacon, lard, feathers, cider, butter, cheese, potatoes, apples, salt, whiskey, beeswax, and bear and deer skins.

eastern part of the territory. Their presence caused tension between the French and the British. This tension eventually led to the French and Indian War (1754–1763). Different American Indian groups helped both countries fight against their enemies.

A year before the war ended, King Louis XV made a secret agreement with King Charles III of Spain. In this agreement, called the Treaty of Fontainebleau, Louis gave New Orleans and Louisiana west of the Mississippi River to Spain. The land was a reward for helping France fight Britain in the war. During the French and Indian War, Spain had lost the Floridas, along the Gulf of

Mexico, to Britain. The gift of New Orleans and Louisiana was not equal to Spain's real losses, but Spain took the land.

In 1763, Britain won the war. France no longer owned or ruled any territory on the North American continent. The Treaty of 1763 stated that Britain owned Canada and all the French territory east of the Mississippi River south to the Gulf of Mexico except New Orleans. The treaty also took West and East Florida from Spain and gave them to Britain. Britain considered Louisiana to be worthless and did not mind that Spain owned it.

CHARLES the III.
In the Robes of the New
from the Original Picture of Antonio Velasquez
KING of SPAIN &c.
Order of Carlos Tercero.

King Charles III of Spain received New Orleans and Louisiana from France through a secret treaty.

British Power in North America

Spanish law did not allow British traders to enter West Louisiana. But Spain did not enforce this law. Some British traders ran successful businesses in New Orleans and West Louisiana. British boats, called floating stores, sold food and supplies to people in New Orleans and villages along the Mississippi River's west side. The Spanish feared the British and were angry with them. Yet the Spanish depended on the British for many of their goods.

The American colonies wanted to be free of British power. The American Revolutionary War began in 1775. During this war, Spanish colonists in New Orleans supplied the American forces with guns, ammunition, and supplies. With support from the Spanish and the help of France, the Americans won the war and their independence from Britain.

The 1783 Treaty of Paris

The Revolutionary War ended with the 1783 Treaty of Paris. Britain gave the

United States all lands south of Canada, north of the Floridas, and east of the Mississippi River. According to the treaty, the Mississippi River was now the boundary between Spanish Louisiana and the United States. Spain would still run the river, but it would be open to all United States citizens.

King Charles III of Spain was happy with the treaty. Spain received the Floridas back from Britain and controlled the Gulf of Mexico's shores. Spain claimed more land on the east side of the Mississippi as far as the Ohio River.

The signing of the Treaty of Paris in 1783 (right) officially ended the Revolutionary War.

Chapter Two

Making Treaties

Spain soon began to fear America as much as it had feared Britain. Spain considered Americans intruders because many of them headed west to farm, hunt, trade, and begin new lives. No major roads connected the western territory to large eastern cities. So Americans used the Mississippi River for transportation and trade. They moved their products through New Orleans and across the Gulf of Mexico, to reach the ports along the Atlantic.

By 1784, the Spanish had had enough. Spain had priceless silver mines in Mexico, and the country was afraid Americans were getting too close to them. Spain threatened Americans by violating the 1783 Treaty of Paris. Spain closed the lower Mississippi River, no longer allowing Americans free rights to use it or the port of New Orleans.

The Spanish government had other problems than the threat of American settlers. During the French Revolution (1789–1799), Spain had to deal

Without use of the Mississippi River, American traders would have to travel over rough trails, mountains, and forests. The situation made Western American settlers angry.

with new rulers in France. The new French leaders did not like that the country had lost Louisiana to Spain in 1762. They wanted Louisiana back.

The United States Signs Treaties

In 1793, Edmond Charles Édouard Genêt arrived in the United States to represent France. His goal was to conquer Louisiana using the United States as a base. Genêt tried to get Americans to join him. But President George Washington and Secretary of State Thomas Jefferson issued a proclamation of neutrality. This document stated that Americans could not aid France or any other country.

Spain wanted peace with the United States. Spain knew that the United States and Britain had signed an agreement called the Jay Treaty in 1795. Spain saw the treaty as a threat to its control of Louisiana. In 1795, Spain and the United States signed the Treaty of San Lorenzo, or the Pickney Treaty. In the treaty, Spain guaranteed Americans the right to freely use the lower Mississippi River and the port of New Orleans for three years.

Both treaties made France nervous. Britain, France's enemy, and Spain both had peace and power in North America. France reacted by seizing American ships and stopping trade with Britain. In 1797, the United States was pushed into an undeclared naval war against France, called the quasi war.

The French Revolution brought new rulers to power in France.

Chapter Three

Napoleon's Plan

In November 1799, Napoleon Bonaparte came
to power in France. He and a group of French
leaders called the Directory overthrew the previous
government of France. Then Napoleon forced the
Directory out and ruled France alone as a dictator.
As a dictator, Napoleon was more powerful than a
king. His goal was to conquer the entire world.

Peace with the United States was important to
Napoleon. He signed a peace treaty with the United
States in September 1800, ending the quasi war. But
Napoleon had other plans. The day after signing the
peace treaty with the United States, he arranged to
have Louisiana transferred from Spain to France.

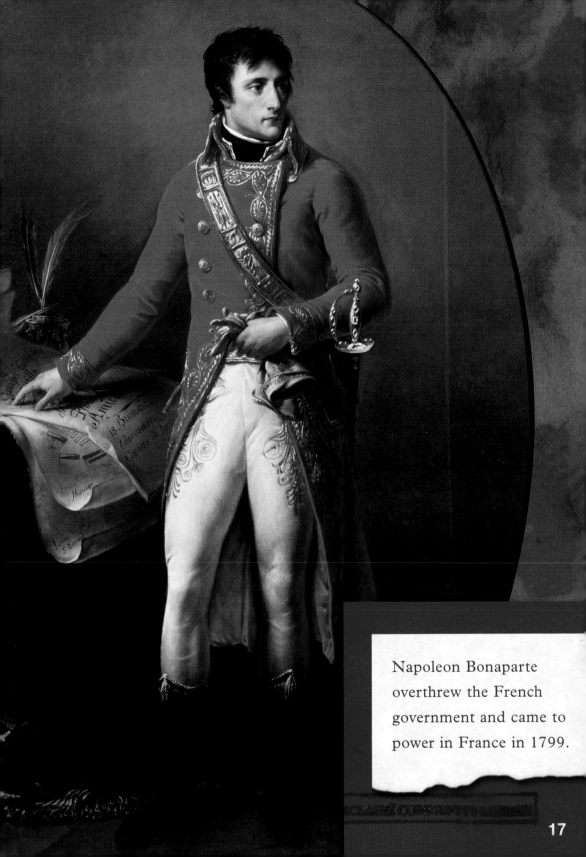

Napoleon Bonaparte overthrew the French government and came to power in France in 1799.

Napoleon's Roots

Napoleon was born in 1769, on Corsica, an island in the Mediterranean Sea. France controlled Corsica. By his early 20s, Napoleon became involved in politics on the island. He and his followers disagreed with Corsica's current governor. But the governor's forces were stronger than Napoleon and his followers. In 1793, Napoleon and his family were outlawed from the island, and they moved to France.

Treaty of San Ildefonso

Plans for the transfer began when Napoleon suggested a deal to the Spanish royal family. Napoleon offered land in French-controlled Tuscany to King Charles IV and his wife, Queen Maria Luisa. This land in Northern Italy would be named the Kingdom of Etruria. Napoleon promised that the king and queen's daughter and their son-in-law, Luis, would rule this new empire. In return, Napoleon wanted Spanish Louisiana.

The agreement between Napoleon and the king and queen was settled in October 1800. It was called the Treaty of San Ildefonso. Napoleon made another promise to the king and queen. He would not sell or give away Louisiana to any other nation.

Napoleon did not keep his promises. Luis and Maria Luisa never had power in Etruria. Instead, Napoleon's armies and generals controlled both Etruria and Louisiana.

King Charles IV (in black coat) and his family gave Louisiana to France in return for control of the Kingdom of Etruria.

St. Domingue

Napoleon planned to occupy Louisiana soon, but he had one thing to take care of first. Napoleon planned to take complete control of St. Domingue in the West Indies. Today, this country is called Haiti. St. Domingue was one of the world's richest colonies. It provided two-thirds of France's total products sold. These products included coffee, sugar, cotton, and indigo, which was used to make blue dye. Napoleon believed this colony, along with Louisiana, would be the key in his plan to control world trade.

Napoleon put his brother-in-law, General Victor Emmanuel Leclerc, in charge. Napoleon gave Leclerc instructions to take control of St. Domingue. Leclerc was to remove the colony's leader, Toussaint L'Ouverture. Napoleon wanted his brother-in-law to restore slavery in the colony. After that, Leclerc was to make his way to Louisiana to build the French Empire.

Toussaint L'Ouverture

Toussaint (below) was born into slavery in 1743. He was freed at the age of 47. Soon after, Toussaint became a major leader in the slave uprising against the French government in St. Domingue. As a result of the slaves' fight, the French ended slavery in St. Domingue. Toussaint became president of St. Domingue in 1801 after freeing the colony from French control. The French called Toussaint "a villain" and a "serpent."

Things did not go as Napoleon planned in St. Domingue. Even after the French captured Toussaint in June 1802, his followers continued the fight. Many of Napoleon's men died from a disease called yellow fever. In 1803, the French were forced to surrender.

Robert Livingston tried to find out if New Orleans and West Florida were available for purchase.

President Thomas Jefferson

In 1801, Thomas Jefferson became president of the United States. Soon after taking office, Jefferson heard a rumor that Spain had returned Louisiana to France through a secret treaty. This news worried Jefferson. He had hoped to buy the land on the Mississippi River, including New Orleans, for the United States.

Jefferson had recently appointed his friend Robert Livingston as the minister to France. Jefferson asked Livingston to find out the truth about the treaty. If the transfer was not official, Jefferson wanted Livingston to try to discourage the French from taking Louisiana. If the trade had occurred, Livingston was to negotiate with France for New Orleans and West Florida.

Livingston was able to speak only with Charles Maurice de Talleyrand-Périgord, Napoleon's minister of foreign affairs. Talleyrand denied that any treaty had been signed between France and Spain. Months passed, and Livingston became frustrated because the French would tell him nothing.

Chapter Four

Jefferson Senses a Threat

In November 1801, Jefferson finally saw a copy of the Treaty of San Ildefonso. The paper confirmed that Spain had given Louisiana to France. Jefferson feared having Napoleon's troops so close to the United States, controlling New Orleans.

Already, Spain had taken away the right of Americans to store their goods in New Orleans, as promised in the Treaty of San Lorenzo. Thousands of American westerners relied on this right for economic survival. Some were so dependent that they threatened to be loyal to whatever country owned New Orleans. The United States prepared for a possible war with France.

Thomas Jefferson (below) had dreamed of increasing the United States' size. Even before the Louisiana Purchase, he planned to have the West explored. On January 18, 1803, he asked Congress for $2,500 to send an expedition into Louisiana's unexplored areas. He wanted to know about its land, animals, plants, and American Indians. He also wanted to know if there were any river routes to the Pacific Ocean.

James Monroe

In January 1803, Jefferson asked James Monroe to be minister to France and join Livingston. Monroe owned land in the West. Choosing Monroe to negotiate with the French showed that Jefferson was taking the concerns of western settlers seriously. Jefferson gave many instructions to Monroe. He told Monroe that it was up to him to keep the peace.

James Monroe (right) went to France with instructions from Jefferson to keep the peace.

Jefferson's Worry

Jefferson was uneasy when he found out that Spain had given Louisiana to France. Jefferson wrote to Livingston, "The day that France takes possession of New Orleans . . . we must marry ourselves to the British fleet and nation." Jefferson was afraid of Napoleon's plans and believed the United States would need help to survive against him.

Monroe left for France in March 1803. Jefferson told him to offer up to $9,375,000 for the purchase of New Orleans and West Florida, if Napoleon refused to sell New Orleans alone.

Jefferson told Monroe that if the French did not accept this offer, Monroe should make a demand. He was to ask that all Americans receive full rights to navigate the entire Mississippi River. Monroe also was to see that Americans be allowed to store their export goods in New Orleans. If Napoleon rejected these demands, Monroe was to go to Britain. Britain had offered to join the United States in a fight against France. The two countries would prepare to take Louisiana back from France.

Chapter Five

A Big Change in Plans

Napoleon had expected his fleet of ships in St. Domingue to continue on to Louisiana. In December 1802, Napoleon learned that yellow fever had killed his brother-in-law and much of his army.

In Holland, ice trapped the French ships that Napoleon had planned to send to Louisiana. Napoleon still ordered the fleet to sail in March 1803, when the ice would melt.

Meanwhile, King George III of Britain learned of the buildup of Napoleon's fleet in Holland. King George assumed that these French ships were headed toward the British Isles, not Louisiana. Napoleon knew if his ships kept going it would mean a battle with the British. He knew he could not win such a fight with his weakened soldiers. So Napoleon ordered the French ships in Holland to cancel their trip to New Orleans.

King George III of
Britain (above) was a
threat to Napoleon.

Napoleon's Failing Dream

Napoleon now had many problems. He had to deal with the defeat of French troops in St. Domingue. A threat of war with Britain loomed. America was upset with the French occupation of Louisiana. In fact, Americans were perhaps even ready to fight.

Napoleon could not handle another defeat in the Western Hemisphere. So he decided not to occupy Louisiana. He hoped the decision would ease tensions between France and the United States.

King George III (with binoculars) was concerned about Napoleon's plans to conquer the world. The cartoon shows George keeping a close eye on the French emperor.

In the spring of 1803, Napoleon changed plans. He wanted to sell Louisiana. His new goal was to take over the island of Malta. The move would cause war with Britain, and Napoleon would need money to fight. By selling Louisiana, he could raise that money.

On April 10, 1803, Napoleon met with French ministers François de Barbé-Marbois, and Denis Decrès. Napoleon told them it was time to give up hope of a North American empire. It was time to focus solely on expanding his power in Europe.

Napoleon told the men why he wanted to sell Louisiana to the Americans. The sale would help America become France's ally, or friend. The addition of Louisiana and New Orleans would allow the United States to become more powerful than Britain.

Decrès disagreed and urged Napoleon not to sell New Orleans. Barbé-Marbois supported Napoleon. He believed that France should leave North

Communication Gap

In the early 1800s, there were no telephones, faxes, e-mails, or other forms of quick communication. A message could take up to two months to travel from France to the United States. Monroe and Livingston were afraid Napoleon would change his mind about selling Louisiana. They were forced to make a quick decision about the purchase on their own.

America. Napoleon decided to sell not only New Orleans, but also all of Louisiana.

Negotiations

On April 11, 1803, a few hours after Monroe's arrival in France, Talleyrand asked Livingston if the United States would like to buy all of Louisiana. Livingston, surprised by the question, made an offer that Talleyrand considered too low.

Barbé-Marbois asked Livingston the same question, suggesting a price of $20 million. Livingston said the United States had no interest in any land but New Orleans and the Floridas.

Finally, Monroe officially met Talleyrand. After the meeting, Livingston and Monroe offered $8 million for Louisiana. Napoleon was unhappy with the offer. He led the Americans to believe that he might not sell the land at all unless they offered more money. The Americans and French bargained until they agreed on the price of $15 million.

The Americans wanted this deal to include the Floridas, which still belonged to Spain. Barbé-Marbois made a verbal promise to the Americans. He said that the French would pressure Spain into giving the Floridas to the United States.

These photos show the cover of the Louisiana Purchase treaty and the document's first page.

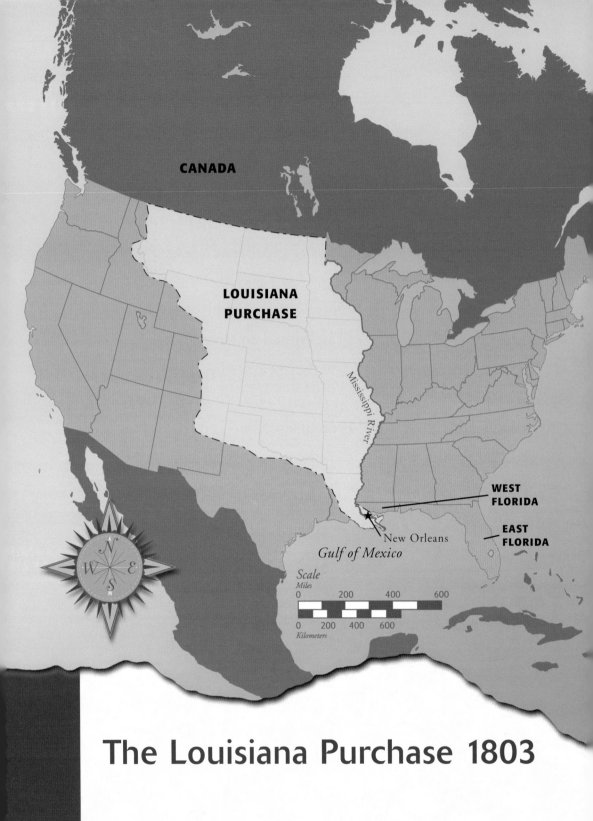

CANADA

LOUISIANA
PURCHASE

Mississippi River

WEST
FLORIDA

EAST
FLORIDA

New Orleans

Gulf of Mexico

Scale
Miles
0   200   400   600

0   200   400   600
Kilometers

The Louisiana Purchase 1803

The Purchase of Louisiana

To protect himself and France, Napoleon made sure that certain terms were met with the Louisiana sale. Napoleon insisted the land become part of the United States. All the land's occupants had to become U.S. citizens. These terms would make the United States stronger. The United States could then help protect France from Britain.

Napoleon also required that the United States favor the commerce and navigation of France. All the ports and towns of Louisiana had to give the French and Spanish freedom to import goods without customs or dues for 12 years. Finally, Napoleon asked that all French debts owed to U.S. citizens be canceled.

Livingston and Monroe had no authority to spend $15 million to purchase any land other than New Orleans and the Floridas. But Livingston and Monroe agreed to the deal. By the first week of May, the agreements were drawn up. On May 1, Napoleon approved the treaty with the United States. On May 2, the papers were signed and predated April 30. Louisiana was purchased!

Chapter Six

Approving the Purchase

When Jefferson heard of the Louisiana Purchase on July 3, he was extremely excited. His dream of western expansion was coming true, and it was happening without war. He also had great confidence that the fertile lands of the West and the ownership of the Mississippi River would strengthen America's economy.

Most Americans were excited about the purchase and the possibilities for expansion, too. The new land meant endless opportunities. But some people were not happy. They saw the purchase as a debt that might put the country into bankruptcy. These people also were afraid that the eastern states would lose governmental and commercial power to the western states. Some feared that if the country became too big, it might not stay united.

The biggest problem with the purchase of Louisiana was whether it was constitutional. As much as the

Meriwether Lewis and William Clark (wearing hats) led an expedition into the Louisiana Territory in May 1804, once the transfer of Louisiana to the United States was official. Their journey lasted more than two years.

sale excited Jefferson, he was worried about it. The Constitution did not specifically give him the power to purchase new land by way of a treaty. But the government did not have time to amend, or change, the Constitution to make the purchase constitutional. Napoleon again was changing his mind. If Congress did not approve the sale quickly, the country could lose Louisiana. So the Senate approved the purchase by 24 votes to 7.

The U.S. Constitution did not state whether new land could be purchased for the country, but it did allow treaties to be made with other nations. At first, Jefferson felt unsure that such a purchase was legal according to the Constitution. Later, Jefferson said that he had "stretched the Constitution until it cracked."

Cash or Credit?

The United States did not have $15 million to spend. In fact, the country already was more than $7 million in debt. The House of Representatives in Congress passed laws allowing the United States to borrow the money to purchase Louisiana. British and Dutch banks lent money to the United States for the purchase. This money had to be paid back in 15 years.

Spain Was Angry

Spain believed Napoleon had betrayed them by selling Louisiana. They insisted that Louisiana still belonged to them. After all, French troops, not the Spanish, still ruled in the Kingdom of Etruria. Napoleon was not keeping his word as stated in the Treaty of San Ildefonso. Napoleon also had broken his promise that he would never sell or give Louisiana to anyone but Spain.

Spain accused the United States of paying for stolen goods by purchasing the Louisiana Territory. The United States declared that this disagreement was strictly between Spain and France. Spain quietly

The Arkansas Flag

The state flag of Arkansas has many stars. The three blue stars below the word *Arkansas* represent the three countries that owned Louisiana: France, Spain, and the United States.

backed down when threatened by a fight with the United States for Louisiana and the Floridas. King Charles IV of Spain instructed his officials to transfer the land to France. Then the French could transfer the land to the United States.

These transfers occurred in New Orleans' main square outside the government houses. On November 30, 1803, the French flag replaced the Spanish flag. On December 20, the American flag replaced the French flag.

Improving a Nation

Jefferson had asked only for New Orleans and the Floridas from the French. Instead, he acquired all of Louisiana. For less than three cents an acre (4,047 square meters), the United States purchased 828,000 square miles (2,144,520 square kilometers) of land from France. This amount of land is larger than many European countries combined.

With the Louisiana Purchase, the size of the United States doubled. Over time, the land from the Louisiana Purchase made up all or part of at least 14 states. These states were Arkansas, Colorado, Idaho, Iowa, Kansas, Louisiana, Minnesota, Missouri, Montana, Nebraska, New Mexico, North Dakota, Oklahoma, and South Dakota.

But the Louisiana Purchase did more than increase the size of the nation. The new land strengthened the country enough to become a world power. Lewis and Clark's exploration of the Louisiana Territory opened up the West to American settlers. The purchase also increased the powers of the presidency under the Constitution.

TIMELINE

René Robert Cavelier, Sieur de La Salle
claims Louisiana for France.

Treaty of Paris ends the American
Revolutionary War; the United States
receives all land south of Canada, north
of the Floridas, and east of the
Mississippi River. Britain returns the
Floridas to Spain.

The French and Indian War
begins. It ends in 1763.

The American Revolutionary
War begins.

The French Revolution
begins. It ends in 1799.

| 1682 | 1754 | 1762 | 1763 | 1775 | 1783 | 1784 | 1789 |

Treaty of Fontainebleau
gives Louisiana to Spain.

The Spanish close the lower
Mississippi River, no longer allowing
Americans or other foreigners free
rights to use the river.

The Treaty of 1763 is signed.

France sends Edmond Charles Édouard Genêt to the United States.

The United States and Britain sign the Jay Treaty; Spain establishes the Treaty of San Lorenzo to keep peace with the United States.

France wages the quasi war against the United States.

Jefferson asks James Monroe to become the minister extraordinaire to France and join Livingston; the Louisiana Purchase takes place.

| 1793 | 1795 | 1797 | 1799 | 1800 | 1801 | 1802 | 1803 | 1804 |

Napoleon seizes power in France.

The Lewis and Clark expedition begins.

Napoleon signs a peace treaty with the United States ending the quasi war. Spain returns Louisiana to France in the secret Treaty of San Ildefonso.

Jefferson appoints Robert Livingston as the minister to France.

Napoleon sends troops to St. Domingue; the French are defeated in 1803.

Glossary

allegiance (uh-LEE-junss)—loyalty to something or someone

alliance (uh-LYE-uhnss)—a friendly agreement to work together

commerce (KOM-urss)—the buying and selling of things in order to make money

constitution (kon-stuh-TOO-shuhn)—a written document containing the basic principles of a government

expedition (ek-spuh-DISH-uhn)—a long journey for a special purpose, such as exploring

floating store (FLOHT-ing STOR)—a boat used for selling food and supplies to people along a river

minister (MIN-uh-stur)—someone who is sent to represent his or her country or someone in charge of a government department

negotiate (ni-GOH-shee-ate)—to bargain or discuss something to bring about an agreement

neutral (NOO-truhl)—not supporting or belonging to either side in a conflict

proclamation (prah-kluh-MAY-shuhn)—an official public announcement

yellow fever (YEL-oh FEE-vur)—an often deadly disease found in warm regions that is spread by the yellow-fever mosquito

For Further Reading

Blumberg, Rhoda. *What's the Deal?: Jefferson, Napoleon, and the Louisiana Purchase.* Washington, D.C.: National Geographic Society, 1998.

Collier, Christopher, and James Lincoln Collier. *The Jeffersonian Republicans, 1800–1823: The Louisiana Purchase and the War of 1812.* The Drama of American History. New York: Benchmark Books, 1999.

Gaines, Ann Graham. *The Louisiana Purchase in American History.* In American History. Berkeley Heights, N.J.: Enslow, 2000.

Gold, Susan Dudley. *Land Pacts.* Pacts and Treaties. New York: Twenty-First Century Books, 1997.

Places of Interest

The Cabildo:
Louisiana State Museum
701 Chartres Street
New Orleans, LA 70116
http://lsm.crt.state.la.us/cabex.htm
The site of the Louisiana
Purchase transfer

James Monroe Museum and
Memorial Library
908 Charles Street
Fredericksburg, VA 22401-5810
http://www.artcom.com/museums/vs/
gl/22401-58.htm
Dedicated to the life and times of
James Monroe, who helped
negotiate the Louisiana Purchase

Louisiana Purchase Historic
State Park
Located where Lee, Monroe, and
Phillips counties meet in Arkansas
http://www.lapurchase.org/park.html
Preserves original land of the
Louisiana Purchase and includes
a monument

Monticello and
Monticello Visitors' Center
P.O. Box 316
Charlottesville, VA 22902
http://www.monticello.org
The home of Thomas Jefferson,
third president of the United
States who was responsible for
the Louisiana Purchase

St. Paul's Churchyard
Tivoli, Dutchess County, New York
Burial site of Robert Livingston,
the U.S. minister to France
who helped negotiate the
Louisiana Purchase

Internet Sites

The Avalon Project—Louisiana Purchase: 1803
http://www.yale.edu/lawweb/avalon/diplomacy/france/frtreaty.htm
Contains the wording of the Treaty of San Ildefonso and many of
Jefferson's notes and letters regarding the Louisiana Purchase

The Cabildo
http://lsm.crt.state.la.us/cabildo/cabildo.htm
Online exhibit of items and images related to the Louisiana Purchase

DiscoverySchool.com—A to Z History: Louisiana Purchase
http://school.discovery.com/homeworkhelp/worldbook/
atozhistory/l/331960.html
Provides an article on the details of the Louisiana Purchase

Louisiana Purchase
http://www.wealth4freedom.com/wisdom/LApurchase.htm
Has information about the Louisiana Purchase, as well as an animated
map of the territorial growth of the United States

The Louisiana Purchase
http://members.tripod.com/~jtlawson
Offers information and a game related to the Louisiana Purchase

National Archives and Records Administration Exhibit:
Louisiana Purchase
http://www.nara.gov/exhall/originals/loupurch.html
Contains pictures of the original document with Napoleon's signature

PBS: Napoleon
http://www.pbs.org/empires/napoleon
Information and a timeline about Napoleon

Index